The
BUSINESS
Side of
DENTISTRY

PART 2

The BUSINESS *Side of* DENTISTRY

PART 2

Accounting, Tax, Retirement

Alan Thomas, CPA

Richard Benner, CPA

THOMAS & FEES, An Accountancy Corporation

Bay City

PUBLISHING, LLC

For more information contact info@BayCityPublishing.com

ISBN: 978-0-9994730-4-7

Edited by Mikel Benton
Cover illustration by Michael Rohani
Book design by DesignForBooks.com

Printed in the U.S.A.

DISCLAIMER

Please Note: Information included in this book is current at time of print and may not apply to your particular situation. If you have questions regarding your income taxes or Social Security benefits, please contact your CPA or attorney.

Contents

Preface

*A*lan Thomas and Bob Fees were college buddies at California State University in Long Beach. After graduation they joined forces and talents to create *Thomas & Fees, An Accountancy Corporation,* one of the leading California accounting firms that specialize in working with dentists. They developed the company based on the assumption that it was far better to become experts in one field than to have limited knowledge in a large variety of businesses. Because they enjoyed working with the dentists they already had in their practice, they put their efforts toward educating themselves about the business side of dentistry.

It's been *over four decades* since Alan and Bob founded the firm. During this time, they have guided hundreds of young dentists through their careers. They have helped them navigate successfully into their first associate positions and, when the time was right, helped them maneuver through the complexities of practice purchase, sale, and eventually retirement.

They understand dentists. Decades of dental contacts assure that clients won't be advised by a professional who has to guess or experiment. Most CPA firms don't know the difference between an oral surgeon, a general dentist, or a periodontist. To the typical CPA, a dentist is just another small business, like a beauty parlor or gas station.

But for the CPAs at Thomas & Fees, understanding the unique challenges of operating a dental business is why they have been so successful at guiding dentists to financial success

When Bob Fees chose to semi-retire a few years ago, Richard Benner, CPA, joined the firm. Because his father, a highly successful dentist, is a long-time client, it's like a member of the family joined the team. Alan says, "It's great to have computer-savvy young talent and a new perspective in the practice."

You can't stay in business serving dentists for forty-plus years without integrity, proven knowledge, and dental know-how. Proudly, *Thomas & Fees, An Accountancy Corp.* has a reputation that is envied in the industry. Our motto says it all: "We want to be partners in your financial success."

Accounting Services
for Dentists

*W*e can help implement accounting systems that are specifically designed for the needs of your dental practice. They are simple and easy to use, and help you pay your bills and keep a handle on your overhead.

Bill Paying: We recommend you utilize your commercial bank and pay your bills online. The bank remits the checks to your vendors, freeing up time for you and your staff. You can also print checks and pay bills the traditional way if you prefer (print and mail).

Payroll: Your payroll can be called into our office, transmitted by computer or faxed into our payroll department. Your employees' net pay can be directly deposited into their individual accounts. Pay stubs are then emailed to the employees. In addition, payroll deposits are made on time and automatically to the taxing agencies. The required payroll reports and employee W-2s are taken care of as well.

Patient Collections: Your patient collections should be entered into your accounting system each day or week by a member of your staff. Then either monthly or quarterly (depending upon the service you attain) a Thomas & Fees accountant will review your financial transactions and make any needed adjustments. As a result, your financial statements are always up to date and available for your use.

Answers To Questions Or Problems: When questions or problems arise, your Thomas & Fees accountant can go online and make the appropriate corrections. This saves more staff time and frustration and keeps your accounting accurate and up to date.

Dental Office Overhead And Leadership: We know that the average general dental office overhead in the western United States is approaching 65 percent. But, after forty-plus years working almost exclusively with dentists, we know that dental office overhead can be kept in the 50 to 60 percent range. It's a matter of being aware of expenses and having the leadership skills to keep overhead under control. If your overhead is at the higher end of the spectrum, you need to determine why. The answer probably has to do with your leadership skills.

There are two ways to handle overhead. You can be an active participant in the process and decide what you will spend each month in each overhead expense category. Or you can pay all the bills at the end of the month and what is left over will become your take-home pay. Your participation in the control of overhead expenses, or your lack of participation, will decide your salary.

Staff salaries are a big-budget item. We often see dentists being "held hostage" by their staffs. It's not unusual to hear a dentist say, "My office manager said she will quit if I don't give her a raise." It's not an intentional takeover by staff members, it's the result of poor leadership. Here's an excellent example of what we mean, taken from an article on the website of Philip L. Kempler, DMD, broker at Thomas & Fees Practice Sales (tfpsales.com).

> Your front office employee says, "I need more help, Doctor. I'm swamped up here."
>
> Do you automatically hire another person, or do you take time to analyze the situation and come up with a solution that keeps your overhead percentages in line? If you don't, you've just reduced your take-home pay. Let me explain. My front office employee told me she didn't have time to make hygiene re-call appointments. And my hygiene schedule was suffering. I could have hired a full-time person and reduced my net by $35,000 per year. But instead, I hired a woman to come in three hours two nights a week, when patients were at home, and do re-call appointments. For an investment of $60 weekly, less than $3,000 per year, I more than doubled my hygiene production and increased patient treatment across the board.

The doctor, in this scenario, took the time to investigate the situation instead of just "hiring a new employee." By doing so, he found a solution that increased his take-home pay instead of reducing it by $35,000 per year.

Don't blame your staff when a situation like this occurs. It's up to you as the leader to keep team members aware of budget concerns, overhead percentages, and practice goals. Good leaders make team members account-able for those numbers by establishing equitable bonus systems and weekly meetings to review the budget. You'll be amazed how much the overhead can be reduced and production increased when the entire team gets involved.

"Everyone should treat the practice like their very livelihood depends on it—because it does."

Many dentists go into practice without any training on how to run a business, and dentistry is a business. The most successful dentists we see are those who took business courses in college, worked in a family businesses before college, took practice management classes after graduation, or worked beside seasoned and highly successful older dentists. If you don't fall into one of those categories, you are not doomed to failure. You simply need to get more education in the business side of dentistry. We're not saying it's easy. On the contrary, it is going to take consistent due diligence to change your ways. But it will be well worth your efforts. A loss of $35,000 per year over ten years is well over a quarter of a million dollars.

Let's talk about budgets. Some folks think "budget" is a dirty word.

"I can't stand to be on a budget. I want what I want *now*!" one dentist told us quite honestly. "I budgeted all the way through college. Now that I make good money, I don't want to feel restricted."

While we can totally understand this dentist's emotional reaction to budgeting, it's just not rational. In all reality, a good solid budget allows you to plan for things you will need in the future, like equipment, office improvements, and continuing education. A monthly and quarterly budget based on percentages allows you to control your expenses and make choices in a systematic way that protects your take-home pay.

What are the percentages for each budget item in the typical dental office? After decades of working with dentists, we've established overhead analysis templates for the various kinds of dental practices. Compare your practice overhead percentages to our templates and you'll quickly determine where your overhead may be out of control. Labor, lab, and supplies are three areas in the practice that can and should be controlled. (See page 7 for details.)

Staff salaries vary depending upon the type of dental office you operate. But in all cases, staff salaries are a big-budget item. Therefore, attention to salaries is key to controlling your overhead. Ask yourself: do you have staff members who have little or no contact with patients? Are there more people working in the front office than producing dentistry? Do you have layers of managers or supervisors? If you answer yes to these questions, you are probably overstaffed.

About lab fees, many dentists have been using the same lab for years. They get in a rut and don't compare lab fees from one lab to another and they don't compare quality. Check out the various labs in your area and compare costs, quality, and service. It could save you thousands.

Supplies is another budget item that deserves close attention. If you're like many dentists, you have shelves loaded with products that are expired and can't be used. That's money down the drain. Put a good ordering system in place to control purchases and avoid waste.

Lastly, pay attention to your practice profit and loss statement (P&L). Those numbers tell a story about your practice. Compare costs for your line items, at least quarterly. Did costs go up? Why? Is production up or down? Why? Are your collections up or down? Why? What was your hygiene production for the month? Even if your practice overhead is just a few points above 55 percent, you have an opportunity to increase your income by thousands of dollars. Controlling costs is a key element in practice profitability.

What makes a good leader? Here are six common traits we have recognized in successful dentists. First and foremost, know what you want from staff and ask for it. Staff members are not mind readers. So make your expectations clear. The best time to do that is when you first hire a person. State clearly, "I expect you to be on time every day, arrive at the office with a smile, and be ready to work. Can you do that?"

Second, delegate. Let go of jobs that can be done by others. Micro-managing team members will drive efficient employees away and keep you from producing dentistry. You are the primary moneymaker in the practice. Don't get sidetracked doing non-production duties. If your employees can't handle the other stuff, then you have the wrong employees.

Third, set a good example. Show respect for your patients by being on time and by arriving at the office in a good mood and ready to work. If you go into the operatory without even looking at the patient's chart, your employees will follow your lead. If you want employees to care about your patients, then exhibit that attitude yourself. Keep home problems from becoming practice problems. Remember, attitude is contagious, good or bad.

Fourth, compliment good behaviors: "I really like the way you spoke to Mrs. Jones and remembered her grandson was coming to visit. That shows patients that we really care." Also, brag about your chairside assistants in front of patients. Compliments make the patients feel like they have chosen the right dental office. "Wow, Susie, nice job cleaning Mary's teeth. They look fabulous!" Who knows, maybe Susie will return the favor and say, "Awesome crown, Dr. DoRight. The color and fit are perfection."

Fifth, look for training opportunities. Show your staff that you care about them by helping them improve their skills. One way to accomplish this is to implement step-by-step management systems and insist that your employees follow them. It is amazing how quickly team members become trained simply by following excellent systems. For example, a good purchasing system for supplies trains employees to make purchases wisely and frees you up to produce dentistry.

Sixth, don't be wishy-washy about making decisions. Procrastination is a stress maker and a time waster. But don't make snap decisions that you'll have to reverse later. When a problem surfaces, take the time to investigate the problem and come up with a good decision. Then stick to it. Remember, decisions must be made, popular or not. If you determine that your patient base needs evening appointments, then do it. That is good leadership.

In conclusion, your leadership skills will impact your overhead and your take-home pay. If you find your leadership skills lacking, rejoice. You have discovered the obstacle between you and your money; you know what you don't know. Take a class online, purchase a leadership CD series and listen to it while driving to and from the office, sign up for a college course on business management. The possibilities are endless.

Dental Practice Overhead Analysis Templates: How does your overhead compare? Are you unsure what the optimum percentages should be for each item in your dental practice overhead? Don't be. In the appendices section of this booklet you will find overhead analysis templates that were compiled by Thomas & Fees, An Accountancy Corp. They were based on practice data collected *over four decades of experience working primarily with dentists*. They can be used to compare your practice numbers to the norm.

Please Note: Expense percentages differ according to the type of practice being analyzed. These templates are the most common dental practices. To download templates for free, visit our website, http://tfpsales.com.

Chapter

2

Tax Services –
Personal and Business

Tax Planning and Projections
Early in the Tax Year

To achieve the maximum tax savings, *you must plan ahead.* Tax planning early in the year allows recommended tax-saving strategies to be implemented. Let me give you an example. If you show up for your income tax appointment in March and have failed to pay your business bills before the end of the year, you must postpone taking those deductions for another year, which can result in additional taxes. If you don't have a plan to make large charitable gifts or harvest stock losses to offset stock gains, you miss deductions again. A little here and a little there can end up costing thousands in unnecessary income tax.

Commonly Missed Proven Tax Stratagies

In addition to the significant tax-saving opportunities outlined in the retirement section of this book, there are additional tax-saving strategies that we often see missed. What follows are just a few of the tax-saving strategies we recommend when applicable.

HIRING YOUR CHILDREN: If you put your children on your payroll to do legitimate work in your dental practice, you may deduct their salaries from your business income as a business expense. If your child is under eighteen, you won't have to withhold or pay any FICA (Social Security or Medicare) tax on the salary, subject to a couple of exceptions. This allows you to transfer part of your business income from your own tax bracket to your child's tax bracket, which should be much lower than yours. This maneuver can result in big tax savings.

The Tax Cuts and Job Act (TCJA) has additional benefits. Your child will have to pay tax on the salary you pay him or her only to the extent that it exceeds the standard deduction amount for the year. TCJA has greatly increased the standard deduction. For 2018 and later, it is $12,000 for single taxpayers, up from $6,350 in 2017, making it possible for your child to earn $1,000 per month ($12,000 annually) and owe no tax on the income.

The following chart shows the new, reduced TCJA rates for single taxpayers. As you can see, if you pay your child *more* than $12,000 per year, he or she will only have to pay tax at the new, reduced rates established by the TCJA:

2018 Income Tax Rate	Single Taxpayers
10%	$0 – $9,525
12%	$9,525 – $38,700
22%	$38,700 – $82,500
24%	$82,500 – $157,500
32%	$157,500 – $200,000
35%	$200,000 – $500,000
37%	over $500,000

Under these new rates, your child could earn $21,525 and have to pay a total of only $925 in income tax ($21,525 - $12,000) x 10% = $925.

You must follow the rules

The IRS is fully aware of the tax benefits of hiring a child, so it will be looking at these deductions carefully. If the IRS determines that your children aren't really employees, you will lose the deductions and they'll have to pay tax on their benefits. So follow these simple rules:

Rule 1: Bona Fide Employees

Your children must be bona fide employees, their work must be ordinary and necessary for your business, and their pay must be for services *actually performed*. In the dental office there are many chores that fall into that category: janitorial services, computer in-putting, filing, office exterior and yard maintenance, managing your website, secretarial tasks, such as copying, stuffing envelopes, etc. The key here is common, accepted, and appropriate work for your business. Work done in your home, such as lawn care, house cleaning, or babysitting, does not qualify and is not a legitimate and deductible business expense.

Obviously, the IRS won't believe that an extremely young child is a legitimate employee. What is the age of a child that is acceptable? The IRS has accepted that a seven-year-old child may be an employee; younger than that is probably unacceptable.

Make sure that you keep an accurate record of the hours worked and the tasks performed. We recommend you have your children fill out time cards that include the dates of service and tasks performed. Although not required by law, a written employment agreement is a good idea.

Rule 2: Compensation Must Be Reasonable

The goal when hiring your children is to shift as much income onto them as possible, because they are probably in a much lower income tax bracket. However, the salary must be reasonable. Your child's total compensation (the sum of salary plus all the fringe benefits you provide your spouse, including health insurance and medical expense reimbursements, if any) must be legitimate for the services they provide. The IRS will have no problem if you pay your children what you would another employee for the same task. Don't try paying $100 per hour for secretarial services just to get the deduction. Check with an employment agency and see what the going rate is for secretarial services in your city. Be reasonable.

Also, pay your children just as you do your other employees, monthly or every two weeks. Pay by check, not cash. You will need to prove how much you paid in order to get the deduction. The funds should be deposited into a bank account in your child's and spouse's names. You then have the option to use these funds for a Roth IRA, Section 529 college savings plan or custodial account that you control until your child turns twenty-one.

Rule 3: Comply with Legal Requirements for Employers

Lastly, you must comply with most of the same legal requirements when you hire a child as you do when you hire a stranger. This means you must fill out IRS Form W-4 and complete U.S. Citizenship and Immigration Services (USCIS) Form I-9, Employment Eligibility Verification. You must also record your employee's Social Security number. If your child doesn't have a number, you must apply for one. In addition, you, the employer, must have an Employer Identification Number (EIN). If you don't have one, you may obtain it by filing IRS Form SS-4. You must also complete and file IRS Form W-2 showing how much you paid your child.

Once you are incorporated or have your own practice, you will be able to deduct business expenses.

Deductions for Dentists Just Out of School:

Often overlooked, these are the expenses you incurred to become a dentist. Hand instruments and your library (books you purchased in dental school) can be written off as business expenses. This usually amounts to between $15,000 and $24,000 deducted over several years.

Continuing Education Costs:

Educational expenses can be deducted if they meet either of two tests. The first test is whether the education maintains/improves skills required for business. Examples are a dentist taking a course in some type of new digital x-rays or dental procedure. The second test is whether the expense is necessary to meet a requirement of a regulation or law, an employer requirement, or to maintain employment, pay rate, or job status. Not only are the fees for the educational courses deductible, but travel, meals, car rentals, and hotels are also included. If your spouse is an officer of the corporation or an employee, those costs can be included as well.

Home Office Expense:

If you conduct business at a location outside of your home, but also use your home substantially and regularly to conduct business, you may qualify for a home-office deduction.

For example, if you use your home for preparing treatment plans, returning patient calls, ordering supplies, doing payroll, paying bills, having in-person meetings with patients or vendors in the normal course of your business, even though you also carry on business at another location, you can deduct your expenses for the part of your home used exclusively and regularly for business. This deduction could amount to $7,500 to $15,000, depending upon your business situation.

Accurate and Timely Tax Preparation and Filing—Why you shouldn't file an income tax extension!

At *Thomas and Fees*, we don't file late and we don't file extensions. For the benefit of the client, we file on time because it helps avoid income tax audits. It's been our experience that tax returns filed with the masses get less scrutiny than tax returns filed late. Plus, filing on time saves money in potential fines and penalties.

Also, we don't like surprises! It's just no fun to end up with a big tax bill you weren't expecting. That's another benefit of planning ahead. Unless you have an unexpected circumstance arise, you should know what your tax payment will be, or darn close to it, before April 15th. And because we've used all the quills in our quiver, your bill will be as low as legally possible.

Better Safe than Sorry!

Some accounting firms turn on the money meter every time they pick up the phone. That's great for the accountant, but it's not necessarily good for you. We don't charge you every time we come to the phone. We learned a long time ago that it's far better to have our clients feel free to call than have them make decisions without our input and suffer negative tax consequences later. A quick call or email can often prevent a problem in the making. If you hesitate to ask your accountant's opinion on a decision because you don't want to pay for a charge, then get another accountant. It is better to be safe than sorry or, in this case, pay the tax consequences of being unwilling to pay for a call. *We want to hear from you.*

Chapter

Retirement Plans

Which Retirement Plan is Best for You?

If you are the owner of a dental practice or self-employed, there are several retirement plans, when properly designed, that will meet your specific needs. The enclosed guide can help you evaluate your current plan. **Please note** that contribution limits change on an annual basis and the following examples relate to the 2019 tax year. You may discover that there's a plan better suited to your situation. Don't fret. Making the switch to a new plan is easier than you think. Just give us a call and we'll walk you through the process, at no obligation and no cost. We're here to help.

Defined Contribution Plans: The contributions to these plans are usually defined as a percent of the participant's income. The employer makes the contribution for the employee. Individual accounts are maintained for each employee. The employee accounts consist of employer contributions, earnings, and, in some cases, employee contributions and plan forfeitures. Since contributions, earnings, and other account activity vary yearly, the future retirement benefits cannot be determined. Generally, employer contributions cannot exceed 25 percent of compensation. In addition, some plans allow employees to defer up to $19,000 from their salaries ($25,000 if fifty years old).

Here are factors you need to consider in selecting the right retirement plan.

If You Don't Have Employees

SEP IRA: This plan is easy to set up and maintain. There are no annual funding requirements. Your contribution can be up to a maximum of $56,000 or 25 percent of compensation or 20 percent of net schedule C. There are no government forms (5500) to file and the annual maintenance cost is low.

Simple IRA: This is a combination plan. Employees can defer from their salaries and the employer can match only up to 3 % of the employees compensation. The contribution can be 100 percent of compensation up to $13,000, or if over forty-nine years old, up to $16,000. No government forms to file and low cost to administer.

Self-Employed 401 (K): You can make a salary deferral of 100 percent of compensation up to $19,000, and if over forty-nine years old, up to $25,000. In addition, your contribution can be 25 percent of compensation, for a maximum of $56,000. There are no government forms until the plan assets reach $250,000.

If your spouse participates in the management of your dental practice and receives a salary, then you may double the deferral. For example, your salary is $150,000 and your spouse has a salary of $25,000, your tax-deductible deferral and contribution would be $75,500, if over the age of forty-nine, then $81,500. If both are over forty-nine years of age, $87,500.

Defined Benefit Pension Plan: This type of pension plan promises the employee a specific lump sum or monthly benefit at retirement. The formula is based upon the employee's age, earnings, and length of service. The older you are, the more you can contribute. This plan does not work well for employers with employees who are older and highly compensated. These plans are best used by employers with no employees other than the owner and spouse. For example, a doctor earning $500,000, age forty-eight, with a salary of $250,000 can contribute $250,000 to his plan.

If You Do Have Employees

Now there are other considerations; mainly the cost of covering employees and administrative costs.

SEP IRA: This plan requires that the owner contribute the same percentage to all eligible employees that the owner contributes to his own account. This is generally not the best when you have employees.

Simple IRA: Salary deferral can be up to $13,000, and $16,000 if over forty-nine years old.

There is a mandatory contribution by the employer amounting to a 100 percent match of the first 3 percent deferred by the employees. This plan is generally cost effective because it allows the owner and spouse to contribute $25,000 to $31,000 per year, while keeping employee costs at a minimum.

Profit Sharing Plans–Age Weighted: This plan takes into consideration each employee's age and compensation.

If the owners are much older than the rank-and-file employee this could be your plan. The plan provides benefits in favor of older, highly compensated employees.

Profit Sharing Plans–Cross Tested: These plans are used by small employers who want to maximize contributions for owners (highly compensated) and minimize contributions for eligible employees.

401(K) Safe Harbor Profit Sharing Plans: These are the most popular and flexible plans today. Employees can benefit from these plans even if employers make no contribution. The employee contributions are 100-percent vested at all times.

The plan sponsor and spouse and all employees can make elective deferrals up to 100 percent of their salaries up to $19,000 each, if over forty-nine years old, $25,000. Eligible employees receive approximately 4 percent of compensation as a safe harbor contribution. The plan has annual administration costs and setup fees. This plan allows the owner and spouse to each defer and contribute approximately $44,000 if their salaries are $100,000. The employee costs would be approximately 4 percent of employee salaries. This plan has a one-time setup fee and annual administration costs, which are both tax deductable.

Health Savings Accounts: This is not a retirement plan, but it works just like one. You as a family can deduct $7,000 per year for your HSA contributions and $3,500 if you are single. You get a tax deduction for the contribution. The earnings on the fund are not taxable when earned. When you take the funds out for medical costs or medical insurance, the proceeds are not taxable.

Roth Plans: These plans generally work best for young employers in lower tax brackets. There is no deduction for the contribution and no tax when withdrawn at retirement. 2019 contribution limits are $6,000 and $7,000 if you are 50 years or older.

As you can see, an owner of a dental practice or self-employed dentist has a number of retirement plan options. Which is most beneficial will depend upon the needs of the owner or self-employed dentist.

The following guide can help you evaluate your current plan and compare it to other plans. If you determine that another plan is a better option for you, just give us a call. Making a switch is easy and much preferable to living with a plan that doesn't work for you.

What Should Your Pension Service be Doing for You?

Your pension service should

- ▶ Design your retirement plan based upon your needs and employee census
- ▶ Obtain government approval ensuring your plan meets all federal regulations
- ▶ Work with you and your financial advisor to determine the level of contribution that meets your financial goals
- ▶ Prepare employee account statements, vesting schedules, and account balances at year-end
- ▶ Prepare all required government forms annually
- ▶ Ensure accurate trust accounting

- Reconcile trust accounts
- Allocate earnings, contributions, and forfeitures
- Prepare employee loan documentation processing
- Distribute calculations for terminated or retired employees

▶ Assist and resolve IRS and DOL audits

▶ Prepare required plan amendments

What Your Pension Service Should *Not* Be Doing

We believe it's a conflict of interest for your pension service to recommend, select, sell, or manage your investments. Those decisions should be made between you and an independent advisor.

A quick commercial:

Thomas & Fees Pension Services was founded in 1988 to help dentists traverse the complexities of retirement plans and administrate employee benefit plans. We offer the services mentioned above and we *do not* recommend, select, sell, or manage investments. We leave those decisions up to you and your personal financial advisor.

IF YOU HAVE QUESTIONS, WE HAVE ANSWERS! Feel free at any time to contact us with questions, ask for more information, or receive a free evaluation of your retirement plan or a new plan.

THOMAS & FEES PENSION SERVICE, INC

The plan you choose has a significant effect on your benefits and the employee costs
The following four plans compare the cost and benefits of each plan. As you see in the examples below, choosing the wrong plan can be costly.
The Simple IRA and 401 (k) DEFERRAL comes from the employees' wages.
The MATCH is the employers' cost.
The 401 (k) MATCH is estimated at 4%
The plan example requires 1000 hours worked to be eligible.

Retirement Plan Summary — Simple Ira & Profit Sharing

Employee Census			❶ Contribution		❷ Contribution
			Simple IRA		Profit
	Hours	Annual			
Description	Worked	Salary	Deferral	Match	Sharing
Owner (Over 49 Yo)	2000	$150,000	$16,000	$4,500	$37,500
Spouse	2000	$26,000	$13,000	$780	$6,500
Owners' Contribution				$34,280	$44,000
Front Office	2000	$55,000	$1,800	$1,650	$13,750
Hygiene	800	$40,000			
Hygiene	1200	$60,000	$5,000	$1,800	$15,000
Chair Side	2000	$40,000	$9,000	$1,200	$10,000
Chair Side	2000	$40,000	$3,600	$1,200	$10,000
Employers Cost of Employee Contribution				$5,850	$48,750

Retirement Plan Summary - 401 (K) Two Types

Employee Census			❸ Conribution		❹ Contribution	
			401 (K) Safe Harbor		401 (K) Profit Sharing	
	Hours	Annual				
Description	Worked	Salary	Deferral	Match	Deferral	Match
Owner (Over 49 Yo)	2000	$150,000	$25,000	$6,000	$25,000	$31,000
Spouse	2000	$26,000	$19,000	$1,040	$19,000	$5,200
Owners' Contribution				$51,040		$80,200
Front Office	2000	$55,000	$1,800	$2,200	$1,800	$11,000
Hygiene	800	$40,000				
Hygiene	1200	$60,000	$5,000	$2,400	$5,000	$12,000
Chair Side	2000	$40,000	$9,000	$1,600	$9,000	$8,000
Chair Side	2000	$40,000	$3,600	$1,600	$3,600	$8,000
Employers Cost of Employee Contribution				$7,800		$39,000

Thomas & Fees Pension Service, Inc
Annual Dollar Limits for Retirement Plans

	Maximun Salary	Maximum 401 (K) Deferral	401 (K) Catch-Up Contribution	Maximum Defined Contribution	Maximum Defined Benefit Contribution
For The Year 2019	$275,000	$19,000	$6,000	$56,000	$220,000

	IRA	IRA Catch-Up	Sep-IRA	Simple IRA	Simple IRA
For The Year 2019	$6,000	$1,000	$56,000	$13,000	$3,000

The catch-up amounts apply to participants age 50 or older.
The 401 (K) Deferral can be 100% of compensation up to the deferral limit.
The defined contribution can be a maximum of 25% of compensation up to $56,000.
The combination of 401 (K) deferral plus profit sharing can not exceed $56,000

The Defined Benefit contribution depends on the participants age and compensation.
Generally, the Defined Benefit works best for Owner and spouse only, no employees.
Defined Benefit participants generally should be over 48 years old.

Appendices

Dental Practice Overhead Analysis Templates

How does your overhead compare? Are you unsure what the optimum percentages should be for each item in your dental practice overhead? The following Overhead analysis templates were compiled by *Thomas & Fees, An Accountancy Corp*. They were based on practice data collected *over four decades of experience working primarily with dentists*. They can be used to compare your practice numbers to the norm.

Please Note: Expense percentages differ according to the type of practice being analyzed. These templates are for the most common dental practices. To download templates for free, visit our website, http://tfpsales.com

Thomas & Fees

Overhead Analysis Template
PRACTICE WITH SOLO DENTIST
Appendix A

Office of:_____
Month of: _____

	PERCENTAGE		AMOUNT	
STATEMENT OF INCOME	Optimum	Actual	Current Month	Year to Date
Accounts Receivable				
Production	100%			
Collections	95% - 98%			
Expenses				
Salaries - Hygienist	5% - 9%			
Salaries - Staff	14% - 17%			
Payroll Taxes	2%			
Lab	8%			
Professional Supplies	6%			
Rent & Utilities	8%			
Office Supplies & Computer	3%			
Legal, Accounting & Collection	2%			
Telephone	1%			
Insurance	2%			
Group Ins. & Employee Benefits	2%			
Advertising	1%			
Other Business Expenses	4%			
Maintenance				
Promotion				
Education & Seminars				
Dues & Subscriptions				
Equipment Rental				
Licenses & Permits				
TOTAL EXPENSE	60%			
NET CASH INCOME	40%	%	$	$

Thomas & Fees

Overhead Analysis Template
PRACTICE WITH ASSOCIATES
Appendix B

Office of:_____
Month of: _____

STATEMENT OF INCOME	PERCENTAGE		AMOUNT	
	Optimum	Actual	Current Month	Year to Date
Accounts Receivable		_____	_____	_____
Production	100%	_____	_____	_____
Collections	95% - 98%	_____	_____	_____
Expenses		_____	_____	_____
Salaries - Associate	5% - 10%	_____	_____	_____
Salaries - Hygienist	5% - 9%	_____	_____	_____
Salaries - Staff	14% - 17%	_____	_____	_____
Payroll Taxes	3%	_____	_____	_____
Lab	8%	_____	_____	_____
Professional Supplies	6%	_____	_____	_____
Rent & Utilities	4%	_____	_____	_____
Office Supplies & Computer	3%	_____	_____	_____
Legal, Accounting & Collection	1%	_____	_____	_____
Telephone	1%	_____	_____	_____
Insurance	2%	_____	_____	_____
Group Ins. & Employee Benefits	2%	_____	_____	_____
Advertising	1%	_____	_____	_____
Other Business Expenses	8%	_____	_____	_____
Maintenance				
Promotion				
Education & Seminars				
Dues & Subscriptions				
Equipment Rental				
Licenses & Permits				
TOTAL EXPENSE	70%	_____	_____	_____
NET CASH INCOME	30%	_____ %	$ _____	$ _____

Thomas & Fees

Overhead Analysis Template
ORTHODONTICS PRACTICE
Appendix C

Office of:_____

Month of: _____

	PERCENTAGE		AMOUNT	
STATEMENT OF INCOME	Optimum	Actual	Current Month	Year to Date
Collections	100%			
Expenses				
Salaries - Staff	17% - 22%			
Payroll Taxes	2%			
Lab	1% - 3%			
Professional Supplies	6% - 9%			
Rent & Utilities	5%			
Office Supplies & Computer	3%			
Legal, Accounting & Collection	1%			
Telephone	1%			
Insurance	2%			
Group Ins. & Employee Benefits	2%			
Advertising	1%			
Other Business Expenses	4%			
Maintenance				
Promotion				
Education & Seminars				
Dues & Subscriptions				
Equipment Rental				
Licenses & Permits				
TOTAL EXPENSE	50%			
NET CASH INCOME	50%	%	$	$

Thomas & Fees

Overhead Analysis Template
ORAL SURGERY PRACTICE
Appendix D

Office of:_____
Month of: _____

	PERCENTAGE		AMOUNT	
STATEMENT OF INCOME	Optimum	Actual	Current Month	Year to Date
Accounts Receivable				
Production	100%			
Collections	98%			
Expenses				
Salaries - Staff	14% - 20%			
Payroll Taxes	3%			
Professional Supplies	8%			
Rent & Utilities	8%			
Office Supplies & Computer	3%			
Legal, Accounting & Collection	2%			
Telephone	1%			
Insurance	2%			
Group Ins. & Employee Benefits	2%			
Advertising	1%			
Other Business Expenses	4%			
Maintenance				
Promotion				
Education & Seminars				
Dues & Subscriptions				
Equipment Rental				
Licenses & Permits				
TOTAL EXPENSE	50%			
NET CASH INCOME	50%	%	$	$

Co-authors of the book, Alan Thomas and Richard Benner

Thomas & Fees Accountancy Corporation is a Tustin, California-based CPA firm that has been working almost exclusively with dentists for over forty years.

Alan B. Thomas, CPA, is the President and co-founder of Thomas & Fees Accountancy Corporation. He is a graduate of California State University at Long Beach and holds a BS in Accounting and MBA.

Richard C. Benner, CPA, Partner, joined Thomas & Fees Accountancy after a career with the public accounting firm PricewaterhouseCoopers (PwC) in the real estate and consumer products assurances practices. Richard holds a Bachelor of Accountancy from University of San Diego and lives with his wife, Kristine, in Costa Mesa, California.

Thomas & Fees, An Accountancy Corporation
Alan Thomas, CPA, and Richard Benner, CPA
Tax Accountants and Advisors
511 East First Street
Tustin, CA 92780
714-544-4341 FAX 714-731-7296
athomas@thomasandfees.com
rbenner@thomasandfees.com

www.ingramcontent.com/pod-product-compliance
Lightning Source LLC
Chambersburg PA
CBHW071525210326
41597CB00018B/2897